How does it feel . . . ?

How does it feel . . . ?

BY JOYCE STRAUSS

WITH ILLUSTRATIONS BY SUMISHTA BRAHM

HUMAN SCIENCES PRESS
72 Fifth Avenue   3 Henrietta Street
NEW YORK, NY 10011 ● LONDON, WC2E 8LU

Published in 1981 by Human Sciences Press
72 Fifth Avenue
New York, NY 10011

Library of Congress Cataloging in Publication Data

Strauss, Joyce, 1936-
    How does it feel...?

    Reprint of the 1979 ed. published by Velvet Flute
Books, Los Angeles.
    SUMMARY: Presents 40 questions intended to
stimulate discussion of feelings.
    1. Emotions—Juvenile literature. [1. Emotions]
I. Brahm, Sumishta. II. Title.
[BF561.S76 1981]   152.4   80-29673
ISBN 0-89885-048-7

This book is dedicated to my children, Beverly, Karen, and Dan, who are my teachers and my friends.

. . . and the sun brings forth a new sound
that fills the air;

a sound so clear
and pure
to reach each living form with daring force
providing warmth in tone,
and light in song,

and so surrounding all
with the bright perfection
of each breath taken,

and each life shared.

How does it feel . . . ?

How does it feel . . .

when you smell a flower?

How does it feel . . .

when you sing?

How does it feel . . .

when the wind blows?

How does it feel . . .

when you have to eat something you don't like?

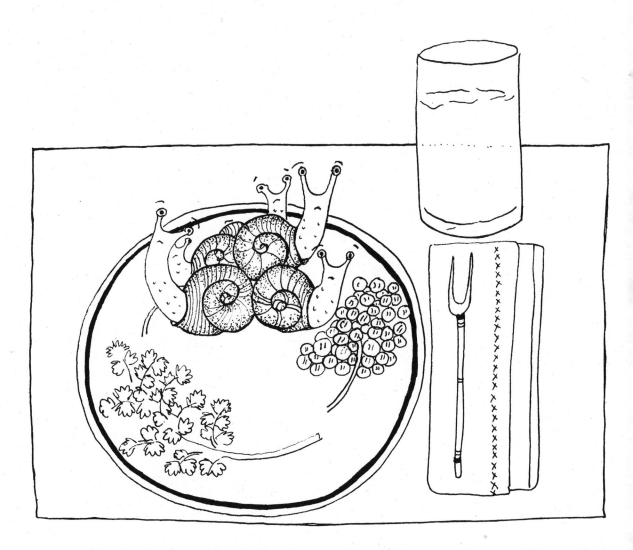

How does it feel . . .

when you are alone?

How does it feel . . .

when you see your reflection in the mirror?

How does it feel . . .

when you finish a project?

How does it feel . . .

when someone tickles you?

How does it feel . . .

when something dies?

How does it feel . . .

when you hug?

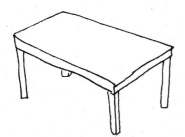

How does it feel . . .

when someone says you're cute?

How does it feel . . .

when you lose something precious?

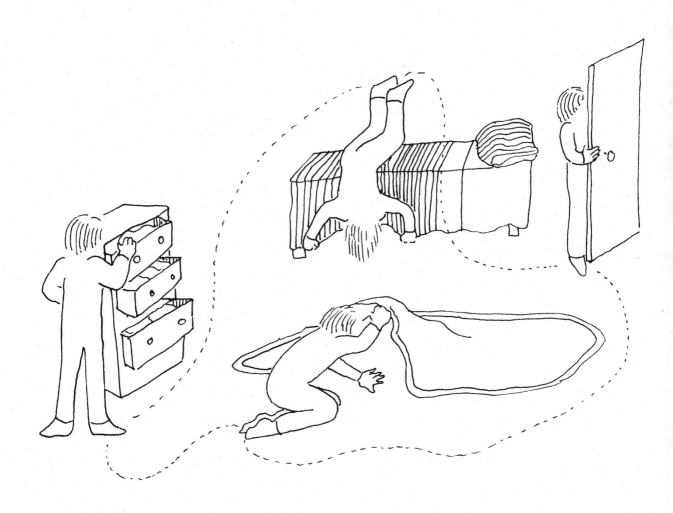

How does it feel . . .

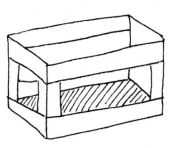

when no one listens to you?

How does it feel . . .

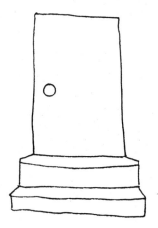

when you meet someone for the first time?

How does it feel . . .

when you do something you're not supposed to do?

How does it feel . . .

when you see a bee?

How does it feel . . .

when you're sick?

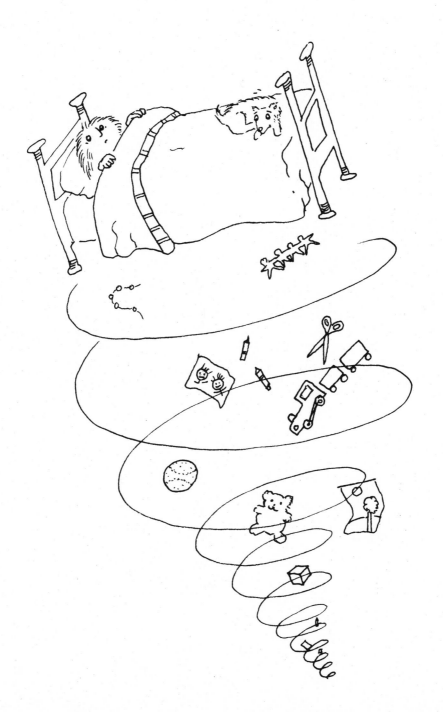

How does it feel . . .

when you hear music?

How does it feel . . .

when you are left out?

How does it feel . .

when you cry?

How does it feel . . .

when someone takes something from you without your permission?

How does it feel . . .

when you're blamed for something you didn't do?

How does it feel . . .

when you receive something new?

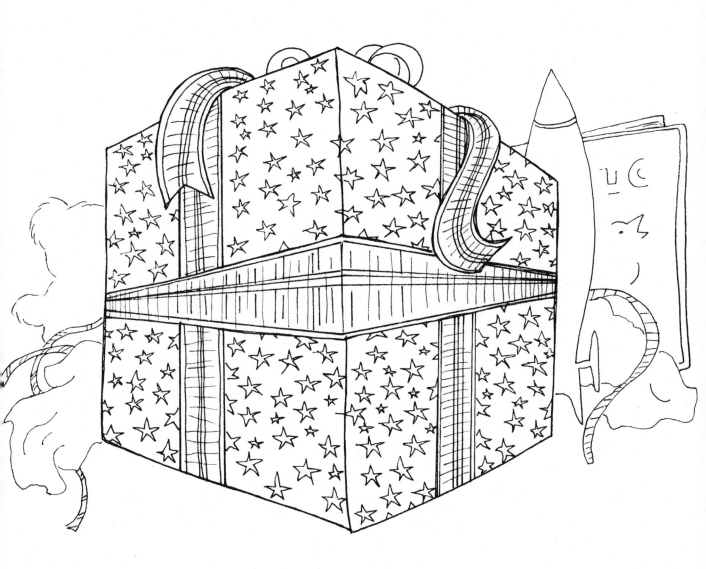

How does it feel . . .

when you don't know the answer to a question?

How does it feel . . .

when you win?

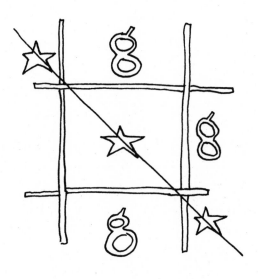

How does it feel . . .

when you're told to eat when you're not hungry?

How does it feel . . .

when it rains?

How does it feel . . .

when you are yelled at?

How does it feel . . .

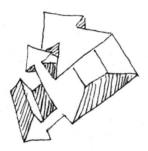

when you're constantly told what to do?

How does it feel . . .

when you look at a sunset?

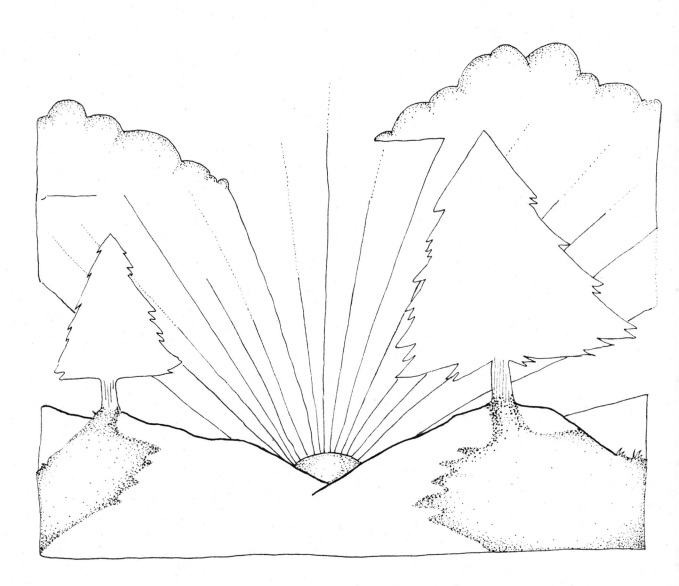

How does it feel . . .

when someone says, ''I Love You''?

How does it feel . . .

when someone touches you?

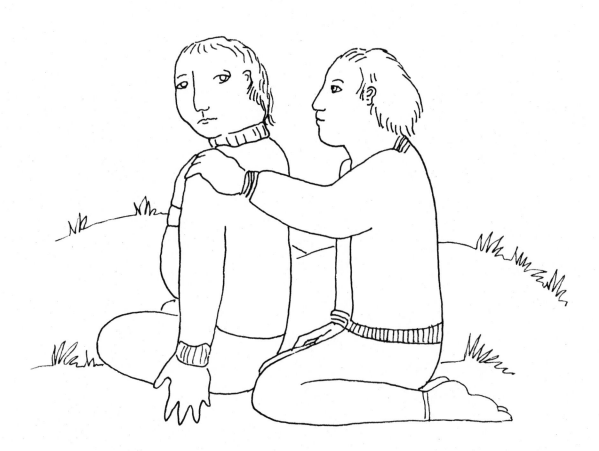

How does it feel . . .

when you kiss?

How does it feel . . .

when it's dark?

How does it feel . . .

when someone makes fun of you?

How does it feel . . .

when someone tells you to go away?

How does it feel . . .

when a puppy licks your face?

How does it feel . . .

when you play?

How does it feel . . .

when you get praised?

How does it feel . . .

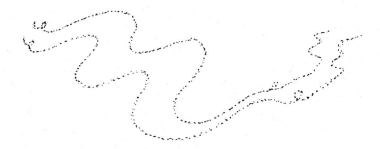

when you have fun?

ACKNOWLEDGMENTS

My deep appreciation and love to my sister Hilda Rubay, and to my friends and relatives Dick Berman, Perry Botkin, Jr., Gil Garfield, Bernie Safyan, Jack Doner, Max Rubay, Louis and Julie Strauss, Vida Freeman, Susan Nathanson, Judy Leach, Charles Isenberg, Arthur Hoffe, George Moed, Allan Shoff, Florence Kohn, and to my mother Pearl Strauss, for their continuous encouragement, help, and support.